RUSTING RELICS OF MINNESOTA

EVADING THE CRUSHER

JULIE BRONSON

AMERICA THROUGH TIME®
ADDING COLOR TO AMERICAN HISTORY

America Through Time is an imprint of Fonthill Media LLC
www.through-time.com
office@through-time.com

Published by Arcadia Publishing by arrangement with Fonthill Media LLC
For all general information, please contact Arcadia Publishing:
Telephone: 843-853-2070
Fax: 843-853-0044
E-mail: sales@arcadiapublishing.com
For customer service and orders:
Toll-Free 1-888-313-2665

www.arcadiapublishing.com

First published 2020

ISBN 978-1-63499-232-9

Typeset in Trade Gothic 10pt on 15pt
Printed and bound in England

CONTENTS

ACKNOWLEDGMENTS

I WOULD FIRST LIKE to thank Doug, my husband of nearly four decades, for keeping the love of cars, tractors, and other wheeled things in my heart and life for so long. Second, thank you to my friend, LeAnn, for always wanting to go on an adventure with me, even if it is to a rusty junkyard. I also need to thank my friends, Susie and Kathy, who help me dot all my i's, cross all my t's, and untangle the words I throw together.

I would especially like to thank the people who gave me permission to wander around and photograph their treasures.

INTRODUCTION

I GREW UP WITH a junkyard in my back yard. I learned early on to look for goodies hiding under the seats when a new car was dragged into the lot. I found plenty of change, a few toys, and more pocket combs than you can count. There is always something salvageable on an old relic. The metal trim and emblems on cars are like gold to some people. Not only do people look for these items to use on their cars, they are also used for wall art. I've had gobs and gobs of grease on my hands and dirt under my fingernails that just wouldn't wash off. Doug and I could have a motor pulled from a car before it had a chance to cool off, drop another one in, and be back on the road again before nightfall. It is the love of all things motorized that I hope to bring to you in this book.

Sometimes, while looking for motorized rust, I find things just as beautifully rusted that didn't have a motor, so I take shots of them as well. I would much rather see a car sitting with trees growing up so close they are hugging it than see it go to the crusher. I am probably one of only a few people that likes to slow down going by an old salvage yard. I hope you enjoy this jaunt with me through a few of the places where most people see scrap, not treasure.

RUSTING RELICS OF MINNESOTA

EVADING THE CRUSHER

I GREW UP AROUND cars. From as far back as I can remember, I was cleaning a car, driving a car, getting parts for a car, or helping someone fix a car. I'm not one to do my own fixing, though I will help as much as I can. I know the basics like changing a tire, which I have done quite a few times out on the road, be it freeway, gravel road, county blacktop, or parking lot. I can also change the oil if I need to.

But as much as I have been around the nice shiny ones, I think I love the rusty old relics left sitting in long forgotten places more. Individual specimens are lurking everywhere imaginable. They are hiding in groves of trees, totally swallowed by vegetation all summer, along fence lines, and sometimes even sitting right out in the open for years and years, longing to be put back into service.

Junkyards are a special kind of treat for me, as there are so many different sorts of cars, trucks and buses. Each one has its own story to tell. In this book, I am only attempting to show the beauty I see in the rust and clouded or missing windows, as well as the fine lines the older cars and trucks used to have "when cars were cars." I am not attempting to identify any of these old cars. If you happen to notice a few more Pontiacs than anything else, well, that is because I love Pontiacs! A few of my own cars will make their way into this edition. I hope they are fun for you to look at and bring back many memories. Maybe you will recognize some of the vehicles shown here.

Abandoned pickup sitting in front of an abandoned house in Alma City.

Here is a '58 Chevrolet Delray tucked away in the weeds. I am not sure if it has been there for so long it has sunken into the ground, or whether the ground has risen up to it.

Almost missed seeing this one near Waseca.

Fuel filler door on a classic old Pontiac GTO. Pitted chrome and rust at its best.

Above left: This one was a workhorse from day one. It was used as a lumber truck.

Above right: Lumber truck then tow truck. Hard life for this one.

This old Bonneville came to us with a dent in every body panel. I hit a deer with it one night, and it came up over the hood, hit the windshield, and went up over the roof. It didn't total the car!

I have also found a lot of other types of transport or working-type machines to include in this book, such as equipment that worked itself to death or was driven to the point of total exhaustion and just gave up. There are a few tractors and other farm implements included as well.

A lot of the rust is caused by time and the fact that the paint has been stripped away by years of weather. Much of this is caused by the salt used on the roads in the winter in Minnesota. Salt is extremely corrosive to these cars and we have been using salt for many years.

It almost made it to the barn before the snow came near Mankato.

Headlights built right into the grill of this Ford pickup by Harmony.

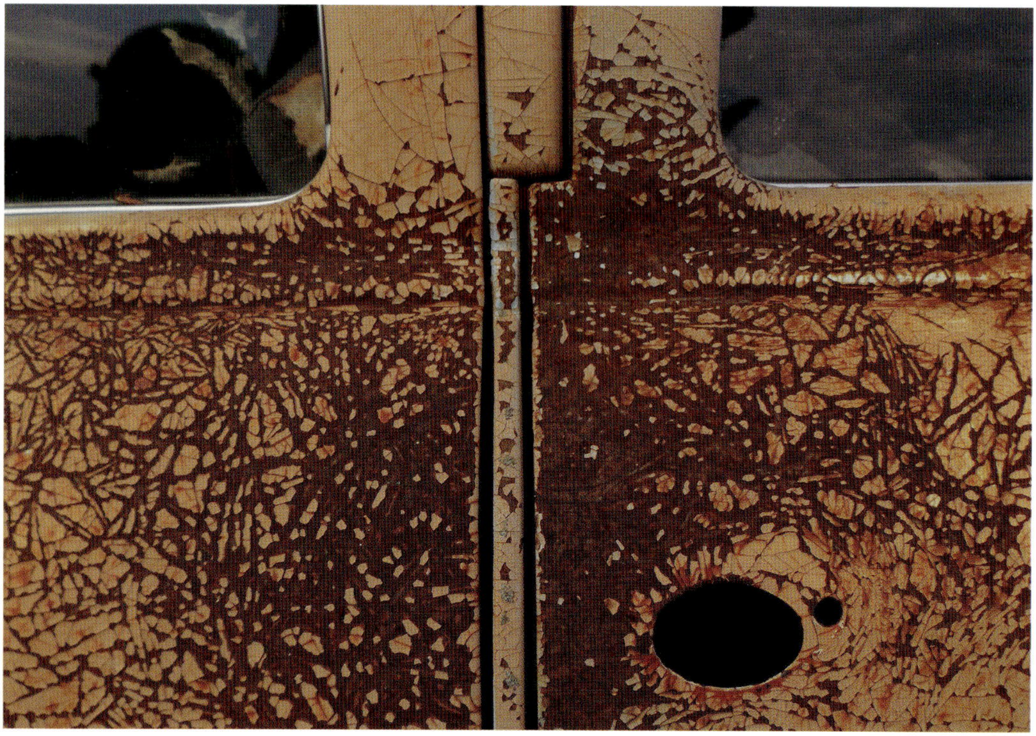

I wonder if a little wax would make this shine. Maybe I will have to use rubbing compound.

I wonder how long this one has been sitting here on blocks near Geneva.

To begin, I will take you for a walk in a salvage yard close to home. We (my husband, Doug, and I) fix up old Pontiacs. We have several we've restored, so naturally, we need to have some donors stored away to use their parts if necessary. A few of the donor cars have actually become restored cars. We also use them as a reference when putting cars back together. I can't tell you how many times we have walked back in our inventory to grab a bolt or hunk of trim that was needed for another project. This car collection has been both a source of parts and inspiration for me, as I can often be found out there taking pictures of it in all kinds of weather. I have been outside when my fingers were freezing until I almost couldn't feel them any longer, and when the sweat was dripping and the skeeters were biting so ferociously I was going nuts, but I had to have that good shot!

Am I the only one who sees ice teeth?

Above left: A beautiful Bonneville in winter.

Above right: Too bad to use, and too good to scrap. It must be in pickup purgatory.

One wonders how many years it takes to bake the paint completely off like this.

I think this Pontiac Firebird was a project someone started and didn't finish near Glenville.

Believe it or not, this car is on the road today racking up a few miles on its own power. Sometimes things aren't as far gone as they appear.

Some cars have been through way more than any car should be subjected to. A mad dad rolled this one around with a bulldozer.

Even when covered in snow, you can still tell it is a Pontiac.

This old truck was one of our first acquisitions. I remember taking it to an auction and bringing home an old Minneapolis Moline R tractor in the back of it, along with an old mission-style fold-out loveseat/bed. We also hauled home approximately 100 loads of gravel for our driveway from about 3 miles away. When we no longer had a job for it to do, we parked it out back. We didn't have the heart to junk it, because it still ran. It probably would now if we gave it a little time and love.

The old International Harvester truck was also one of our first workhorses. We used to use it to pull motors, trees, a stump grinder, and even a garage back to our home. It was cast aside when it was no longer useful. Now, it too sits, waiting to be loved again. I can't believe some of the stuff we used to work with when we were young.

This little Tempest was brought home in 1983, and it sat growing trees until we decided to restore it. When we were getting ready to pull it home from about fifteen miles away, we discovered a nest of hornets and a nest of bumblebees in the back seat. Doug's job was to ride, and mine was to pull; however, I was nervous and killed it in the middle of the road, and we nearly caused an accident, so we switched places. I rode in the Tempest with the hornets and he drove the truck. Unfortunately, the door wouldn't latch, so we used a bungee to hold it shut, and I kid you not, I almost went nuts because of the possibility of getting stung, so I took the bungee off the door and held it shut the rest of the way home.

This is one of my favorite photos. It is a '65 Bonneville that my husband owned back when he was in high school, then sold or traded for other wheels (as a guy sometimes does). He sold it and acquired it again about three times. We were at a tractor pull, at a farm over near Austin, MN, when we saw it sitting in the field, so of course it had to come back home to stay. It has been a great sunset and snow prop for me.

We put many miles and hours on this old workhorse. It had a boom on it for pulling motors, lifting garages, or any other thing that needed to be hoisted up. We pulled a stump grinder all over the area too for a while. It is now getting a well-deserved rest.

This is my old GMC nestled in the vegetation.

Above: We had to cut the trees down to rescue this one. It is now painted and gets driven every summer.

Right: Love those stacked headlights!

Our neighbors have a little truck body sitting at the top of their driveway. They decorate it for the changing seasons, so I try to get up there when they do to get a photo or two.

My father-in-law had a couple of cool looking old vehicles up at his place that were picture worthy. One was an old Pontiac. They had the neatest hood ornaments. Sometimes they were lit. He also had a cabover body GMC that was mighty pretty. Now that we have discussed some of the local treasures, we can travel further afield.

We'll begin our road trip at a junkyard that has been around as long as I can remember and is only a few miles from us. It is between Gordonsville and Glenville on Highway 65, about five miles north of the Minnesota/Iowa border. This "boneyard," as we call it, sits in an old gravel pit. It often floods so badly that you can't see the cars down in the center. There is a gravel road that runs past it, so you can get a good view from above.

I went to this junkyard with my husband, Doug, looking for parts for one of our cars, since the yard changed hands. It used to be owned by a grumpy old guy who we didn't get along with, so we didn't buy parts from him. I will give you an idea how mean he was. About forty years ago, Doug and this man made a deal to buy a trunk lid off a '55 Pontiac. Doug didn't have time to take it off that day, so he told him he would come back with tools on Saturday. When he went back on Saturday, the man had literally moved a few cars out of the way to get to the '55 Pontiac and crushed it. Luckily, a guy named Bob who worked there knew of another one for Doug. He never went back, and always told people that if that guy had the only part in existence that would make his car go, he would learn to ride a horse. He doesn't like horses! Thankfully, now it has a different owner and that grumpy guy has passed on.

My neighbor's yard art.

The neighbor's yard art decorated by nature.

Neighbor's yard art in summer.

I was trying to get a photo of the old granary, but the GMC photobombed me.

Right: This is one of my favorite parts of the old cars. This would have been a lighted hood ornament. It's so sad that they don't do this anymore.

Below: A tired old shell of a motorcycle left to rot in the weeds.

Weeds sneak in, even behind the emblems on this Oldsmobile F85.

I wonder if the fence is so people can't get in, or so the cars can't see out. This is M2, Misgen's salvage yard near Gordonsville.

A good place to pick up a pickup. Near Gordonsville.

I wandered around with my trusty old Pentax, snapped a few shots, and got permission to return with my friend when I had time. There are some odd things laying out in old junkyards, such as projects people begin, but don't finish, and ideas that may have sounded good at the time but didn't quite work out the way they planned. Mostly, you find cars and trucks that have met their fate either by a crash or mechanical failure. After that, parts get sold off from them to make others complete. You can't just go to the store to buy new bumpers or doors for the old beasts.

I love going to junkyards just to feel the vibes these old relics throw off. I often wonder about the people that owned them, and how many miles they put on them on summer vacations or trips to visit their grandparents with the kids. Back then, you would stand on the seat by the driver or lay in the back window in the sun and take a nap. I remember those days. It seems like the roads were narrower and the speed limit was much faster, too.

Twin H Power. If I remember correctly, this was a Hudson near Gordonsville.

Prairie Gold painted pickup near Gordonsville.

A unique car with others stacked on top of it near Gordonsville.

Snowed in for winter.

Many of the cars have been here for decades. More are added as farm places are sold and cleared out. The junk guy will come and buy whatever is out in the grove to bring back here to sell parts. Unless, of course, there is absolutely nothing left of them, then they go right to the crusher. Iron prices are very low right now, so they make more money selling parts if they can find a buyer. There is also a huge trend with "rat rods," which is a car or truck people will fix up to run and drive, but they don't make them pretty. In fact, they make them look as bad as they can and use many unusual items for parts. Most have little or no paint. You don't need much to start. A rusty body can be set on a newer frame that has good running gear and brakes, and away you go.

Some of the unique details on these old gems really make a person appreciate the time and talent it took to design the classics of days past. The portholes on an old Buick said, "I am a Buick!" and the bullet-style hood ornaments on a Chevy said, "I am a Chevrolet!" The stars of decoration on the quarter panels of a Pontiac said, "I am a Pontiac!" Details such as these set them apart from the others, even though the body style was usually enough to give away the make and model. They still felt the need to add these marks of distinction.

Above left: The open door on this sedan seems to be waiting for someone to hop in and go for a ride.

Above right: Early grill guard. Apparently, deer have always been an issue.

Savoy by Plymouth. I like how the emblem has protected the paint close to it.

Above left: I'm not sure what this one is, but the tree and the blue sky set it off nicely.

Above right: I first thought this looked like a huge spider.

This old truck, though rusting, is still being used for farm work near Keister.

Classic Buick portholes.

Seeing how the paint has faded differently on the front clip and the rest of the car makes you wonder if there was body work done in the past and the paint ingredients didn't match on this big beautiful Pontiac.

Imagine my surprise to find this hiding in a shed near an old abandoned house. It has been rescued by someone.

I am a cat lover, so I had to get a picture of this one.

Ford truck in the bushes near Le Sueur.

Pontiac Starchief stars.

The glass that is left unbroken in a few of these old vehicles has great fogging and bubbles in it. The frames of the windows make for a unique way to frame a shot, too. A jagged edge on broken glass is fun if you're careful.

Next, we visit an abandoned farmyard owned by a friend. One of the coolest busses I have ever seen is here. It's a throwback to the futuristic look they must have been trying to achieve back in the 60s or 70s (I think, as I don't really know what year this behemoth was made). It must have been mighty fancy back when it was new. It would be fun to make a camper out of this one to travel around in.

Looking through both back windows on this old coupe makes the pickup cab in the distance stand out.

Foggy window shot. This is one of my favorites! Near Gordonsville.

I love taking shots of old glass, whether bubbled, frosted, damaged by a gunshot, or broken. It all adds character.

Above: The frosted edges on the glass are a nice contrast to the green moss growing on the rubber weatherstrip.

Right: Corner window view of the dash of the blue pickup.

This old purple bus has quite the futuristic look. What a hoot it would be to fix it up and travel.

An Oldsmobile Toronado keeping the bus company near Twin Lakes.

I love the shape of the cab on this old International truck near Twin Lakes.

I am thinking this was a farmer's Ford put out to pasture near Twin Lakes.

Not too far away from the bus is a pair of old draglines. They were used to dig ditches and basements and such. I saw these a couple of years ago just sitting out in a field. It appears they are growing old together. They sit close enough to keep each other company in their long retirement years. A few miles away is another one sitting alone in retirement. There are also old hunks of iron so covered in vines that you must study them to make out what they are. See the street sweeper under all the vines? The vines grow inside the tractor cab, too. Apparently, it doubles as a terrarium.

It's always fun to find an old relic that the trees are trying to take over. Trees grow wherever they please and form around all parts of any car, truck, or implement. They trap their victim so tight that it would take a chainsaw to free them, along with a lot of work. Cars and trucks sink down into the dirt so badly that the floor pans rest on the ground and rot away. Luckily, if you have a notion to restore a beauty in that condition, there are new floor pans available to weld in where the old ones were, or you can find a good metal fabricator to make new floors.

Two more old draglines. It is amazing there are three like this within a few miles of Twin Lakes.

A dragline for ditch digging north of Emmons.

This is a vine covered street sweeper.

I think there might be a skid loader and a tractor in those vines. This is a good example of how nature tries to reclaim all.

The tractor cab doubles as a greenhouse or terrarium.

Bad hair day?

Above left: Tree hugger. Or is it a hugger tree?

Above right: A tree grows where a tree wants to grow.

The trees are really wanting to hold this one tight for a long time.

I think the trees are trying to protect it from harm.

The trees haven't found this one yet, but it is sinking. It might be salvageable.

This one was hidden well. I think I would have missed it if my friend, LeAnn, hadn't pointed it out to me.

Just look at how far this one has sunken into the dirt. That doesn't happen in a couple years. It takes a few decades.

I don't think this one is going to roll away.

We'll head up toward New Richland now. My mother's side of the family is from near there. My great grandpa built a house west of New Richland, so we went there to take some pictures. I took photos of this old gas pump. I figured since the rusting relics mostly use some sort of fuel to move about, it would be appropriate to add it. The others on a trailer are at yet another farm some distance away. In a small town near my great grandpa's farm is an old country store turned horse barn. We peeked in the windows. Imagine our surprise to see this Austin Healey sitting covered in bird droppings and sheetrock debris. The old car sits in a garage at an abandoned farm, like someone drove in and parked it after work and never came back.

There is a farm near Waseca that had quite a few of these old cast-iron tanks sitting around. I didn't have a clue what they were, but took multiple photos of them to try to find out later. I finally figured out they were steam tanks from old locomotives or steam-powered tractors. Why this yard had so many of them I will never know, but they were fascinating.

This old gas pump had some neat glass windows in it, but none were unbroken.

I think this is an Austin Healy hiding in an old grocery store turned horse barn.

Old gas pumps. I saw Tin Man when I first saw the one on the left.

Too bad someone felt the need to bust the window out of the back of this old Chevy near New Richland.

Looking in through the broken back window, you can tell the seat cover and visors are still in good condition. Near New Richland.

Heavy cast-iron steam tanks, likely from a huge tractor near Waseca.

Steam tank resting with others like it.

Steam tank stamping. I know it all means something, but I haven't taken the time to research it.

The year on this says 1959, but it seemed older.

Every year on the same day all over the world, usually the first week in October, there is a photo walk. A person from the photography community sets up a location and time, then everyone around the world walks on the same day taking photos. It was my turn to lead a walk, so I chose a place of business that pulls parts from old cars and sells them. Our group had a great time and we all got a few beautiful photos. Many of the people didn't even realize old heaps of rust could be so photogenic. I especially love the far-out upholstery someone chose to redecorate the cab of their truck with, and the shag carpet as a headliner in another. It must have been both warm and noise cancelling, besides being extremely fashionable!

Carpet—it's not just for walking on.

This one has it all. Broken, bent, twisted, rusted, dented, and it still shines!

Decorated by vines.

Perfect patina on a sedan in Albert Lea.

Salvageable Buick emblem. I hope someone saves it!

Above: The chrome and taillights on this beauty would have been stunning at night.

Right: Pretty in pink. Albert Lea.

Woodstock bound?

Corsair by Edsel. Albert Lea.

Travel around in the world!

A Pontiac missing some pieces.

What a perfect planter!

A pickup in this condition sure makes a person wonder what happened. Did a tree fall on it? Did it roll over? We will never know.

Cars stripped of almost everything useful in Albert Lea.

Some of the discoveries I have made have been while out exploring old abandoned farm places. Very interesting things pop up. It almost appears that they have been intentionally hidden from prying eyes like mine, but the shed (or whatever they were hiding in) has fallen, only to nearly wreck the very thing it was trying to protect. Like this tractor and this car. There are so many sentimental reasons for hanging on to these things, but the person who saved it has likely passed on, or in some cases probably forgotten completely about it. Out of sight out of mind, as they say. They will see a car or tractor just like the one they used to drive puttering down the road and say, "Hey, don't I have one of those tucked away out at the farm? I should get that old girl out and get her running." So, the old guy and his grandson go for a ride out to the farm to dig it out, only to find it crushed by a fallen tree or something equally as heartbreaking. It is quite amazing the transformation some of them have gone through if someone does decide to fix them. Restoration is a huge business, which is why these old junkyards are so valuable to have around. You can get some running gear components from a catalog, but many people like to use the original parts if they can. Body parts, even if they are reproduced, are rarely of the same quality.

It is so much fun to look at these old relics and compare them to the equipment in use today. Towing vehicles like this one were just as massive then as they are today. To me, they seem quite a bit more complicated. You can sure tell they meant business!

Left: This is an old gas pump. It would have had a glass enclosure around it.

Below: I bet this was one tough cookie when it was in use. It appears to be a mid-50s Chevy.

International truck.

Peeling paint and faded emblems, yet you can still tell what it was.

Here is an example of good intentions gone wrong. The John Deere was parked in a barn near Twin Lakes for protection from the elements, but the barn gave in before the tractor was used again.

This is an old steel wheeled Case. Imagine what those wheels could do to hot pavement! Near La Sueur.

I have no idea what this is, but it looks complicated to me. Near Waseca.

This dragline is mounted on a truck with a tow bar on the front. How would you like to hook this to the back of your SUV and take it for a pull?

How would you like to see this bearing down on you in your rearview mirror? It would be quite intimidating, if you ask me!

Near Cannon Falls, there's a place where they hold a show every year of all types of motorized things on display. There are demonstrations of all kinds with motors popping away every direction you look. They have on permanent display, serving a purpose, a wall made of cars. It appears to be a gravel pit that has old cars and trucks used to stop the erosion of the gravel. They are beautiful to look at, especially at the "golden hour" when the sun is setting on them. There are also a few along the riverbank and one parked out in the water, as you can see here. They are parked as if they were driven to that point then just left. Kids love it, too.

There is also an area up by Dundas that holds events on Memorial Day and Labor Day weekends. They have flea markets and auctions, as well as threshing demos. At the entrance, they have these threshing machines on display. In 2018, we were there for the Memorial Day flea market and the rain moved in. In its, passing it blessed us with a beautiful rainbow, so I was able to capture this. They changed it now, so that there is only one machine on a newly landscaped mound.

The ducks are wondering what that truck is doing in their pond near Cannon Falls.

Nose on a bulldozer. I love how the Caterpillar is crawling.

A trio of truck cabs at the Little Log cabin near Cannon Falls.

Right: Rusty patina on a sedan near Cannon Falls.

Below: Living on the edge. Or is it dead on the edge? Cannon Falls.

This one appeared to be crawling up out of the pond near Cannon Falls.

Retaining wall of cars and pickups at the Little Log Cabin near Cannon Falls.

A few more years and the paint might be all gone.

Road grader on display at the Little Log Cabin near Cannon Falls.

Above left: Another shot from above the bank on the retaining wall made of cars and pickups.

Above right: Looking down from the upper bank on the dented roof of an old pickup.

Rainbow over the threshing machines at Dundas.

Steel wheels for sale, just in case you have a flat on the way home.

Threshing machine near Dundas.

We must not forget the little things. There are so many bicycles, motorcycles, snowmobiles, tricycles, wheels, and other items left to be reclaimed by nature. They are unrecognizable in some cases, so you must do a double or triple take to see what they once were, but the wheels are a giveaway, telling you to look closer. I had to throw in a few odd items too, like this mailbox. The rusty ones intrigue me. Here you see a sad old wheelbarrow. I guess anything with rust catches my eye.

It seems like so many of the cars or other implements I see are what is left after a good portion of its parts have been removed. Drivetrains were reused for utility trailers or wagons of some sort. Their bodies were left to just rot away. Here we have a wheel that was left, and a tree decided it was a safe place to take root and grow. I don't think even a chainsaw would set this wheel free.

Rusty old mailboxes mounted on an old steel wheel. What is not to like?

Opposite page:

Above: Tricycle just left to rust.

Below: It isn't very often you see a wheelbarrow with an addition. This one had a steel wheel on it too, which would cure the issue I have with flat tires.

Now this might be a rough ride!

Might have to kick this one over a few times before it goes.

This one looks like if there was enough left of it, it would be fun to putter around in.

Am I the only one who thinks this one looks like an owl?

Here is something you don't see every day. I wonder how many years it took to fill it to the rim.

Do you remember wing windows? Back then, it was the only air conditioning you needed, and you could direct it right on your face! I don't drive a car that has air conditioning, so I wish mine had wing windows.

I learned to drive in a '62 Chevy Nova II station wagon with a three speed on the floor, so I enjoy driving almost anything, as long as I know the shift pattern. My first car was a '64 Chevelle convertible. That was traded for a Pontiac as soon as one came along that we were interested in. I remember back in high school, my best friend, Nita, had a mid-60s Dodge Dart. She got a flat tire, so we decided to change it. I knew how to change a tire on a GM car, but the lug nuts on hers were extremely tight. We broke off three of the studs before we realized they were left hand thread on the left side of the car. We thought we were so smart, but we made a bad situation even worse!

Since we are car people, and have been forever, naturally, many of our friends are car people too. Here is a car one of our friends has resting in his backyard. I am not sure if he plans to restore it, or if it will be used for parts for his other car. Another friend has the bubble top Chevy. Notice the tree in the front bumper. They are thinking about restoring it. The tree had to go to get it out.

Snowmobiles are a big part of life in Minnesota. We owned these two, but only rode one of them once a year or so, whether we wanted to or not. We never rode it farther away from home than we wanted to walk back.

Vent windows. The answer to no air conditioning.

To restore or not to restore? Tough decision.

A coworker just brought this home from out of state. Check out the tree that had to be cut away in the front bumper.

I always called these bumble bees. We used to fire one up every year, but never got farther away from home than we wanted to walk back.

Here is a photo of an exposed seat spring covered in ice. Some of the most unlikely things make the most artistic photos. These other photos are also from a rain/ice storm we had. They almost make it look like the car is crying.

As seasons change from dry and cold to hot and humid here in Minnesota, fungus begins to grow on any surface it can. Once it latches on, it is pretty much a self-contained mini ecosystem. It grows slowly, so if you see large patch of it, you know whatever it has attached itself to has been there for a long time. We get a lot of lichen fungus growing on things here. It really adds to the feeling of abandonment.

Tail fins were a huge styling feature back in the day. The Chevrolet ones were especially recognizable, as were the Cadillac fins. Pontiac was a little more subdued, but still you could tell it was a Pontiac. And of course, who couldn't tell a Pontiac beak, even without the crest?

Ice covered exposed seat springs.

Crying taillights on a cold Pontiac.

Nature sure does give us a lot of beauty to work with. As if this car wouldn't be pretty enough!

Abundant greenery.

LP powered Minneapolis Moline with a fine layer of lichen.

Above left: An old Minneapolis Moline missing a couple of teeth.

Above right: That tailfin looks like a cat to me.

Looks like very few parts have been used off this one. Maybe it can be back on the road someday.

Gotta love those tailfins and taillights!

Dramatic tailfin!

I love how the Pontiac emblem stays so bright even after years in the sun.

Classic Pontiac beak—a great style you could recognize from blocks away.

I discovered an old travel trailer and a pickup camper to add to the mix. They don't look like they would have been roadworthy even when new, yet they were! Many miles would have been put on these traveling homes. Now they are used for storage until they, too, fall to pieces. In this case, it doesn't seem like it will be too long of a wait.

It surprises me that an old wooden wheel, such as this one, would still be around after sitting for so many years in the severe weather that we have here. Apparently, good hardwood was used, as pine would have rotted away decades ago, and I rather doubt there was such a thing as pressure treated lumber back then.

I am not sure where this old boat would have been used around here. Someone felt it was worthy enough to save, but it too sits out in a field waiting to be noticed and restored. It would be fun to bring it home to fix up and use as a she-shed!

Coming apart at the seams.

Mobile homes are handy. Don't like your neighbors? Move! House and all!

I remember riding in one of these as a kid. We would watch out the window above the cab.

I have no idea how this wooden wheel can not be rotted away. You would think being out in the elements would have completely weathered it away.

LUNCH
MONEY

I like to photograph the insides and dashes of old cars and trucks. The high-quality materials and protection from the elements ensures their beauty remains. The styling and chrome were very artistic, and some hold their shine as well as their charm.

One of the worst dangers these old cars, trucks, and other implements face is the dreaded crusher. I cringe at the thought. Many times, I have seen a load of squashed cars being hauled down the freeway covered in netting. It is a challenge to try to guess what each vehicle was stacked on or under. Sometimes, you can tell by the tiny bit of fender or trim or a stray emblem that somehow was untouched. Unfortunately, they must go off to be turned in to a soup can or begin a new life as a new car.

Here is what is left of the dash of an old Chevrolet pickup. It must have been a donor for another pickup.

Opposite page:

Above: The tire might be holding air.

Below: A houseboat out in a field near Myrtle.

How's this for a cool old speedometer?

Interior details were just as important as exterior and many times were made to match.

The speedometer on this went up to 80! I can't imagine going over 25 in something like this.

I love how the radio and heater controls match in this old Bonneville.

Another dilapidated dash.

The crusher in the back is what all cars want to avoid. Check out the bugs on that car pile! Near Gordonsville.

Growing up, we had two fuel barrels up on stands. The "gasman" would come when we called to refill the barrels from his tanker truck. It looked like this one, from what I can remember. It was about fifty years ago, so this memory is kind of cloudy. He would bring us Tootsie Rolls and would throw us up in the air and catch us again. He is still just as nice as he was so long ago, although he doesn't try to throw me up in the air anymore.

Whether they are tractors, cars, or trucks, all are gold mines of parts and information. One of the worst parts about seeing all these things at a farm is that you wonder if they will ever get noticed or saved in order to make use of what good is left of them. Often an auction is held. The iron buyers come and just buy the stuff to resell to a scrap yard. They usually don't care about the value of the parts, just the value of the weight. They come in with their cutting torches and chop stuff into handleable sizes, load them up, and haul them away, getting only pennies on the dollar of what the stuff could be worth.

This is what the fuel haulers that came to the farms used to look like. This one is near Austin.

What is left of an old Minneapolis Moline soaking up some sunshine near Glenville.

An old gold Cadillac convertible. The top has rotted away. The body is surprisingly straight on this one.

Cold and lonely, taking comfort in each other's presence.

A collection of pickup cabs waiting to be put to good use.

What was there first—the trees or the trucks?

This old tractor is up to its belly in the earth near Manchester.

Sometime weird things catch my eye. This is a trailer license plate from 1950!

Thank you for reminiscing with me and remember to keep your eyes open and watch for the beautiful old gems hiding away in the woods, farmyards, junkyards and even along fence lines. You never know when you might see a car or tractor that once kept things moving. Maybe it will bring back a long-forgotten memory.

FINAL NOTE

DON'T FORGET TO BE extremely careful when poking around these rusty reminders of the past. There are pieces of metal jutting out and shards of glass just waiting to poke, slice, or peel a layer of skin off. There are also sometimes four-legged critters that set up housekeeping in them and don't like to be startled. Wasps and bumble bees are other residents that, if bothered, will get mad and sting before you even see them. Stay safe and up to date on your tetanus shots. I have intentionally left out the exact locations of most of the relics in this book for obvious reasons, but rest assured they are all in Southern Minnesota, mostly within a forty-mile radius of where I live.

If you enjoyed this book, I have also authored two books about abandoned farms and houses, among many other things: *Abandoned Southern Minnesota* and *Abandoned Northern Iowa*.

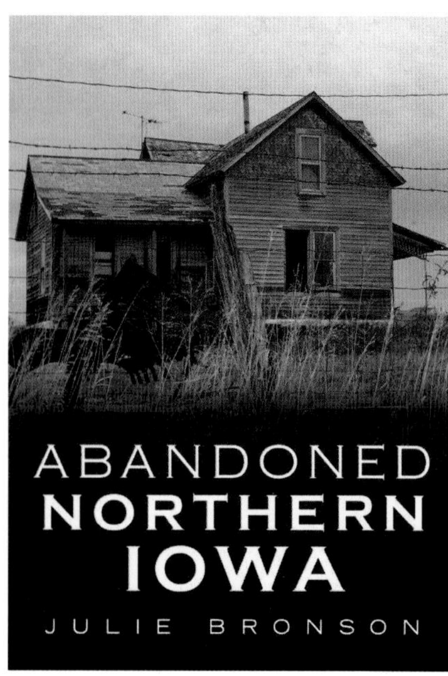